THE NEW ADVENTURES OF DON QUIXOTE

THE NEW ADVENTURES OF
DON QUIXOTE

TARIQ ALI

WITH PHOTOGRAPHS BY ARKO DATTO

Seagull
BOOKS

LONDON NEW YORK CALCUTTA

Seagull Books, 2014

Text © Tariq Ali, 2014
Photographs © Arko Datto, 2014
Director's note © Jean-Claude Berutti, 2014

ISBN   978 0 8574 2 209 5

British Library Cataloguing-in-Publication Data
A catalogue record for this book is available
from the British Library

Typeset by Seagull Books, Calcutta, India
Printed and bound by Hyam Enterprises, Calcutta, India

—— CONTENTS ——

Tariq Ali

REPLY TO THEATRE

AN INTERVIEW WITH TARIQ ALI

You've read Don Quixote *several times during the last 10 years. Do you read different issues out of the text every time, perhaps according to current politics?*

Yes. A masterpiece can be read repeatedly and each time you find new aspects of it—the literary architecture, the use of certain phrases, something that had not been noticed on a first or second reading and, sometimes, the echoes in the present. Above all, it is important to understand that, contrary to academic fashions, great works of literature are rarely, if ever, created in isolation. Nor can they be fully understood outside that given context. They are a reflection of life within a social, political and historical environment. This applies as much to Cervantes and Shakespeare as it does to Joyce and Proust, Goethe and Schiller. And all of them interpret the past with an eye on the present.

What were the difficulties and obstacles, and what were the pleasures and benefits of transferring the ideas of Cervantes' book into our times?

Once I had decided that the best way was to introduce Don Quixote and Sancho Panza as well as their animals into the twenty-first century, it was not so difficult. Economic crises, wars and religion dominate the twenty-first century. So, for me, the pleasures greatly outweighed the difficulties. For Jean-Claude I think it was 50-50, because the play I wrote is not conventional, its style is a homage to the giants of the last century: Meyerhold, Brecht, Weiss. This can be unsettling in today's world, where a monochrome, monotone culture is dominant. Much of what is written is written not to question but to please. This conception is alien to me.

At the Witten/Herdecke University, you gave a lecture called 'Spring is a Short Season—The State of the World'. How do you see our world today in general? Does Don Quixote really stand a chance today?

Here, I will be discussing the state of the world under the domination of a single Empire—the United States. This has never happened in human history. That is why spring can only be short. Cervantes portrayed Don Quixote as deluded in order to protect himself against the Inquisition and he mocked the knight in order to make doubly sure. But all the targets attacked were deadly serious. So, like then, the Don Quixotes of today face very real problems. My one regret is that the revelations about the extent of surveillance over all our lives came too late to include in the play. The Stasi seems a joke compared to the NSA in the US, the GCHQ in the UK and their French and German equivalents. But the new conformity is such that mass anger at these outrages is absent!

What exactly is the role of Sancho? Are there Sanchos in our times?

In the novel, when Sancho is given a chance to govern an insula, his solutions are radical. It is a game, of course, but Sancho takes it seriously. The nobility laughs, but not the reader. It is a hollow laugh. So Sancho is there to prevent Quixote from going too far. Interestingly, in his farewell letter to his children, Che Guevara compared himself to Quixote, writing that he hoped his Rocinante would survive the travels.

If Don Q and Sancho came to Germany, what would they encounter?

Don Quixote has deservedly been called a universal novel, even the first modern novel produced in Europe, but it was, and could only have been, written in the Spain of Philip II, a century after the triumph of the Reconquest and when the country was beset with crises of every sort. The triumphalism generated by 1492 had long worn off. The modern Reconquest was the defeat of communism as well as many of the utopian ideas associated with it. The absence of an enemy, however, has also torn the mask off capitalism. We see its real face all over the world. Germany has weathered the storm better than its EU partners and its EU underlings, but this is not permanent. Within the mainstream, there is no fundamental difference between the two main parties and their Green understudies. The tragedy of the 1968 generation in Germany is most visible in the Greens: pro-war, pro-nuclear power, pro-neoliberal capitalism. Frightened of their own shadows, running non-stop from their past. This is what our four characters find . . .

Do you have any idea or preconception about Essen and the Ruhr Area?
What could it be like for Don Q here?

One of my earlier plays, *Moscow Gold*, was performed in Essen in the 1990s. So I know the theatre and the city. An industrial city, once a powerhouse of the German workers, now in decline like most other European cities (Manchester, Rouen, etc.), but the cultural victories mean that theatres and concert halls remain subsidized and commercial pressures can be resisted, which is almost impossible in Britain. Don Q would find a safe haven in this cultural space but outside, he would be nervous.

THE THIRD ACT
A NOTE FROM THE DIRECTOR

Resuming rehearsals for Tariq Ali's *The New Adventures of Don Quixote*, it's truly as if a new adventure is beginning. The tensions of June, the difficult script sessions and the hesitations about the play all probably bore some fruit. The 'scenic version' that I prepared during the June rehearsals with my assistant Sarah has great advantages. It is tighter than the original, more effective on stage and, strictly speaking, it doesn't sacrifice any of the play's themes. The tightening of the whole also allows us to integrate the music better, something Tariq conceived as an indispensable element of the play. I must say that in the original version there were too many words to put on stage or to music as compared to the extraordinary economy of images that the play now suggests . . .

As for the play's structure, I eliminated two scenes: the one called 'The Angel of History' and the second called 'The Military Hospital Revue'. Let me explain these cuts. I had in fact asked Tariq to write a scene placing history itself in the abyss, or as a way of admitting that Cervantes' original would be impossible to adapt. Tariq had then invented an angel of history who would bring judgement on what is playing out and therefore be more faithful to the original . . . I actually really liked that scene, but it weighed down the play as a whole. And now I think the humour that emerges from the rehearsals allows us to have this ironical view of the original without insisting or explaining. I tried, nevertheless, to convince Tariq to have the Angel of History (borrowed from Klee and Benjamin) intervene at the time of Don's death, but Tariq didn't want to add it. And so I respected his wishes, but that doesn't mean that while rehearsals are still going on I might not restore a bit of that scene to where it was originally planned (following the scene in the Paris cafe) . . .

The case of the second cut scene is different. It was written at the beginning and turned the place of death—the military hospital of Landstuhl—into a joyful hospice, upon the occasion of the arrival of CNN and an ambassador to bestow the Nobel Peace Prize. The whole scene constituted an essentially attractive 'number', but Tariq had placed it after Sancho and Don Quixote had left the hospital. Because the two protagonists were not present at the festivities, the scene became superfluous. Indeed, since the subject of the play is Don Quixote's view of the contemporary world, and since he is not there to convey his thoughts on the scene, something didn't work . . . This was the main reason for cutting it. The second had to do with the scene's tone. The previous scene showed soldiers in bed singing that they were the envoys of the devil and that they were aware of what they had done in Afghanistan and Iraq. Based on the script, Arturo Annechinno wrote music that was part moving and part ironic, that transports the audience into a nightmarish world (in any event, I hope so) that is perfectly in tune with the description of the surgical butchery that follows the war. But all of this unfolds at a slow pace in an atmosphere like that in which one finds oneself when emerging from a nightmare (I must have been thinking of the famous chapter in Malraux's *Man's Fate* that unfolds in a military hospital in Spain). It very quickly occurred to me that it was a shame to follow this important scene with one of simple political satire, and I have no regrets that I cut it.

These are some of my thoughts as I begin to work on the revised version, both with the actors and the composer in the months of rehearsals before us. Regarding the music, it has become increasingly important as we work on the revision or, rather, it has found its rightful place, sometimes as ironical commentary, sometimes as a completely separate character. What I mean by character is that Arturo and I sought to have Tariq speak in ways other than through words—we tried to put ourselves in his head and discover how, through the strong images he proposes, we could find the right commentary, one balanced between irony and compassion. Because I believe this is the secret of the words in this text (and also what makes it difficult to perform)—it constantly hesitates between adherence and critique, and that hesitation, that dancing from one foot to the other, is probably its main quality. In other words, what created a stumbling block at the beginning of our work (I often heard the actors say: 'the author is writing political satire with pathos') is really a rare element in the way plays are written today. I felt this at the time, but wasn't able either to formulate it or to stage it. The various attempts we have made since

June have put us on the right path. Now we have to give them shape.

To conclude this brief state of affairs, I should say a few words on the scene that remains the most enigmatic—the gathering in the desert of gay Muslims from around the world. The tone of the scene was extremely difficult to establish. Even the set designer, Rudy Sabounghi, who was the first to embrace the general structure of the play, found it difficult, and if you look at his sketches which go back to last spring, you can see that they really don't work, whereas everything else is done tastefully and coherently. There was even a moment during the rehearsals in June when I asked Tariq about the possibility of integrating it into the scene at the hospital, like a Utopia for the dying American soldiers. We rehearsed this Marat/Sade alternative for several days, but it didn't work. In the end, after rereading the complete text for the nth time around the table with the actors, a small glimmer of light appeared. What if we were to act this scene quite seriously . . . I won't say anything more here since we are right in the middle of rehearsals, but I wanted to give this example to provide a sense of how difficult yet secretly coherent Tariq's kaleidoscopic writing truly is—you can't unravel its difficulties except by attempting to put together a stylistic puzzle, for which he obviously provides no clues. And this stylistic puzzle (which I associate with the one set up in *Night of the Golden Butterfly* in which painting is constantly at issue) is also a puzzle of meaning for each scene in that it asks the audience to find coherence in the relationships of complementary images. This is perhaps what makes Tariq Ali's plays so original when compared to other contemporary theatre (which he knows extremely well but isn't interested in joining, that is, compared to which he feels independent and free in a manner rare enough to be noticed). He prefers to work 'through images', a bit like Peter Weiss, a German writer whom Tariq and I often discussed during our long conversations . . .

Jean-Claude Berutti
7 October 2013
(Translated by Teresa Lavender Fagan)

PERFORMANCE NOTES

The New Adventures of Don Quixote premiered on 1 November 2013 at the Grillo-Theater in Essen as *Die neuen Abenteur des Don Quijote*. Funded by the Alfred and Clare Pott Foundation, the play was directed by Jean-Claude Berutti, with a script translated from the English to German by Silvia Berutti-Ronelt and Ulrike Syha.

CAST

Don Quixote
Silvia Weiskopf

Sancho Panza
Jens Ochlast

Rocinante
Ingrid Domann

Mule
Jan Pröhl

Female Banker, Woman in Bar,
Soldier-Woman (Dulcinea),
Workshop Reporter 2
Ines Krug

Husband, Intellectual,
Tattooed Man, Private X,
Young Poet
Tobias Roth

Roma Woman, Angel of History,
Afghan Girl, Workshop
Reporter 4
Anne Schirmacher

Finance Minister, Man in Bar,
Gang Leader, Nobel-Committee
Man, Organizer, Pirate
Sven Seeburg

Publisher, Poet, Workshop
Reporter 3
Rezo Tschchikwischwili

Wife, Bartender, Nurse,
Workshop Reporter 1, Roma Family,
Men, Gang, Beggar, Camera
Crew, Politician, Photographers,
Young Soldier, Chorus
Ensemble (all actors)

PRODUCTION

Director
Jean-Claude Berutti

Set and Costume Designer
Rudy Sabounghi

Assistant Set and Costume Designer
Katharina Heistinger

Music
Arturo Annecchino

Choreographer
Katja Buhl

Dramaturg
Marc-Oliver Krampe

Assistant Director
Sarah Mehlfeld

Prompter
Ursula Robiné

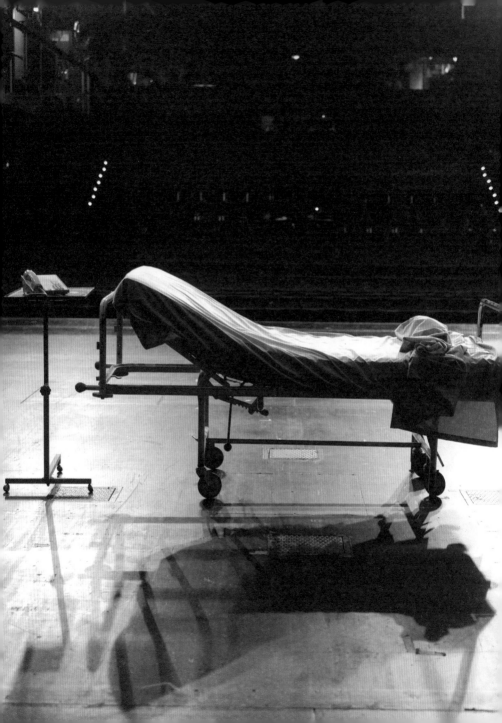

THE NEW ADVENTURES
OF DON QUIXOTE

Roma Woman (Anne Schirmacher),
Wife and Husband (Tobias Roth).

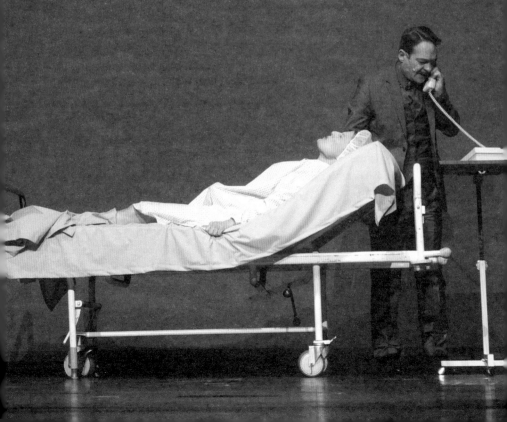

Spotlight on maternity ward. A loving couple. A very pregnant woman, with her husband sitting on the bed stroking her stomach. Roma Woman slides in, cleaning the floor. Husband stares at her in open disgust. Lifts the phone to speak to the matron.

HUSBAND

Matron, let me make it clear. I've already warned you once. She is still here. It's unacceptable. I don't want this Roma whore to be the first thing my newborn child sees when it opens its eyes. Get her out of here.

WIFE

Sounding very tired.
Is this really necessary?

HUSBAND

Shhh. Just rest, my darling. Don't think about anything. I will make sure all goes well.
Glares at Roma Woman.

Roma Woman ignores the talk and finishes cleaning the floor, then rises, smiles at the wife and exits.

WIFE

The waters are bursting.

HUSBAND

Nurse. Come quick. NURSE!

WIFE

AAAH! It's too painful!
She screams and screams.

SCENE 2

Spotlight on Roma Camp. A caravan outside which a family, includ-ing Roma Woman, sits. Music.

ROMA WOMAN
Aside, as she walks to another section of the stage.
I was given the rest of the day off. I was having some coffee in the canteen. A nurse came running. The woman had given birth. The child was born. Was it my fault he was born blind?

Threatening background noises. Men with torches surround the Roma.

MAN 1
We don't want you here. We'll cleanse our country of filth like you. Where's the bitch that blinded the baby?

ALL OTHER MEN TOGETHER
Where's the bitch that blinded the baby?
Burn their balls and kick their guts.
Stick the dynamite up their arse.
Where's the bitch that blinded the baby?

Roma Woman hides behind her grandmother, who is set on fire. Roma Woman runs away. Caravan is overturned. The men chase her off the stage trying to set her on fire.

—— SCENE 3 ——

The clicking of horses' hooves. Spotlight on Don Quixote and Sancho Panza, attired in mediaeval gear, as they ride onto the stage. Sancho is carrying an overweight sack of books on his shoulder. As they dismount, Roma Woman runs across the stage.

ROMA WOMAN

Help, will someone please help? Help me! Help. Help. Help. I've been running through this bloodthirsty continent.

The two men pour the bottles of water they are carrying on her to douse the fire. Sancho takes off his jacket and puts it round her. She is trying hard to control her sobs. Don Q gives her some brandy to drink. Both men fuss over her.

DON Q

Who are you? What happened? Come now, drink some of this. It's real vintage. 1672.

SANCHO

Who did this to you?

ROMA WOMAN

They burnt my grandmother to ashes. They accused me of having blinded a newborn baby in a hospital where I cleaned the floors. All lies, sir.

Don Quixote (Silvia Weiskopf),
Sancho Panza (Jens Ochlast) and
Roma Woman (Anne Schirmacher).

SANCHO

An auto-da-fé, señor.

DON Q

The present always unearths the crimes of the past and reuses
them for its own purposes. Do not worry, my good woman. I
will avenge you with my sword. I will find these rascals and give
them . . . and give them . . . yes, something they will remember.

ROMA WOMAN

I can't stay now, sir. I must run to another country. It must be
written that we can never live in peace. We Roma will never find
peace in Roman lands. My people have lived in this continent for
fifteen hundred years. Fifteen hundred years. And still it goes on.

Thank you for your kindness. I must keep moving.

Exit.

DON Q

Sancho, please go and find the animals. We too should
move soon.

Exit Sancho.

*Music. Don Q is agitated and walks from one end of the stage to the
other, deep in thought. Then he speaks directly to the audience.*
Memories battle in my mind. Burn the heretics. Let's go to Mass.

Then, the auto-da-fé. Three heretics in Seville will go up in
flames. Torture them first. Is he a real Christian? No. He still will
not eat pork. He washes himself five times a day. Burn him. Burn
him. But the witnesses lied, screams the poor devil. They lied,

they lied. The Inquisitor, heartless and with a cold demeanour pronounces: In order to safeguard greater truths, we must be prepared to lie. Lies are necessary if the truth is to be uncovered. Yes, innocents will die. It's the only way. If torture extracts a confession then it safeguards the truths of our world. That's how they spoke when I was born, so many centuries ago. And they still do. Times change, but the capacity of human beings to do mischief to each other has remained constant. Only I can change this world.

Only I can bring justice. Only I can punish wrongdoers.

Sancho returns, leading Rocinante and Mule.

SANCHO
They were busy, I can tell you.

DON Q
Sancho, you must keep that mule under control. If he mounts my Rocinante more than once a day, she is too tired to carry me. Tie the mule's penis to his tail.

SANCHO
Heaven forbid, señor. You speak like an Inquisitor. Can you hear those noises too, or is it just my imagination?

DON Q
Beware of imaginations, Sancho. Remember where they took us in the past—but I think you're right. As the sun sets the noise gets louder.

Darkened stage. Distant noises. A mosaic of sounds. Exaggerated laughter, clinking glasses, mobile phones ringing, sniffing, a hint of sex. Noise fades.

SANCHO

Looking at the sack full of books.

What strange world is this, master? What were those noises we heard? They seemed like people in trouble. We should go and help them, but this time please don't do anything rash. Don't provoke any one or else we'll be beaten up again. My body still bears the wounds of our old adventures.

DON Q

I will try very hard to maintain my composure, but if I lose control you must calm me down.

SANCHO

I'll give you a glass of water and ask you to count to ten before you speak again.

DON Q

And remember, this is a world where you may no longer call me Master . . .

Sancho grins and gives Don Q a familiar slap on his arse. Don Q glares at him.

. . . But you must always behave as if I am. A touch of informality is permitted. A joke or two at my expense, whose aim really is to flatter. Never close to the truth. And never touch me again. Remember, Sancho, underneath the mask of equality there must

be an unmistakable obsequiousness. Nobody must doubt who is
squire and who is Don.

SANCHO

Aside

That will be really difficult.

DON Q

You may dismount.

SANCHO

I already have.

Don Q dismounts. Rocinante, his horse, sighs with relief.

ROCINANTE

Can we go and get some sleep now?

SANCHO

Yes, but a warning. My trusty mule is tired. Don't interfere with
her tonight.

Rocinante snorts in disgust and animals exit.

Don Q (Silvia Weiskopf) and
Sancho (Jens Ochlast).

DON Q

And the same applies to you, my friend. We are in a territory
where such acts will soon be illegal.

SANCHO

Master, I mean, Don Quixote, how long must I carry these
books? My back hurts. My bones ache . . .

DON Q

There are only three I wish to keep. The others should be burnt.

Sancho empties the sack.

DON Q

Getting irritated as he sorts out the books.

We keep Adam Smith, Marx, Vilar and Polanyi. I should read
them again . . . Just look at these absurdities. *Why Globalization
Works* by Martin Wolf, *The Lexus and the Olive Tree* by, by . . .
Oh, it doesn't matter. *In Defense of Globalization* by Jagdish . . .
into the fire. *Globalization at Risk . . . Globalization and its Enemies*
. . . this one *Development and Freedom* . . . is borderline no . . .
Too weak. Here. Finished. Makes me sad that young people are
being taught all this at their universities. Just like those stupid
books on chivalry so long ago. Remember?

SANCHO

What will happen when the young learn these books like a cate-
chism and reality slaps them in the face?

DON Q

A very important question, if I may say so, Sancho. A very important question. Perhaps we will soon discover the answer. Indignation creates *indignados*, as we know from our own country, but where we are now is the heart of our continent. This is where the money supply is controlled.

SANCHO

These days it is impossible to burn books. They don't do it any more. Is that a good thing?

DON Q

Possibly. It would be better if fewer books were published. Fewer but better. Yes, Sancho, fewer but better. We'll get rid of these books. Into the oubliette.

SANCHO

Don Quixote, I found this piece of paper. It says that rubbish can be left in bags on the street corners every Monday and Thursday. Our problem is solved.
He sighs and begins to load the sack again.

DON Q

Mondays and Thursdays. But not Fridays, Saturdays and Sundays. Civilization, at last. They will not disturb the holy days of the Muslims, Jews and Christians. It would have made the Inquisition very unhappy.

SANCHO

But why not Tuesday?

DON Q

Puzzled, then his face lights up.

Holy day of Buddhists.

SANCHO

Aside.

It's an old habit with him, but I always know when he's making things up . . . and before this play is over, you will too.

Rocinante and Mule are lying on the ground, reading.

ROCINANTE

Sometimes he surprises me. Three books he kept. I've read them.
Not bad. But why not this one? Hegel. *The Philosophy of Right.*

MULE

Idealist! I'm reading Rosa Luxemburg.

ROCINANTE

Are you really tired?

MULE

Yes. Go to sleep.

They put down their books and the lights go out.

*Noises of a party now re-emerge and get louder. A section of the stage
begins to light up in anticipation. Don Q and Sancho stand up and
look in the direction of the noise. They can see, but the audience waits.*

DON Q

Observe them carefully, Sancho. How they love the distorting
mirror of their own world.

SANCHO

But can they not see us watching them?

DON Q

Could Narcissus see anything but his own reflection?

SANCHO

I don't know.

DON Q

I posed a rhetorical question. The answer lies in the question.
Why can you never understand that?

SANCHO

I don't know . . . oh . . . sorry. I didn't realize it was another
rhetorical question. But why can't they see us? This is a real
question.

DON Q

Not yet, but . . . just wait . . . Now!

——— SCENE 5 ———

THE STEALTH BANKERS

*Tableau. Music to jangle the nerves—a mix of a Shostakovich quartet
and Schoenberg. The stage is brightly lit. A select party is in progress.
At first it appears as if all of them are playing with themselves but it's
soon obvious that they're texting. Then they're sniffing. They are
bankers, politicians, CEOs, media celebrities and a few tame intellec-
tuals fawning over them. They are both self-absorbed and absorbed in
one another.*

*In the distance, a glimpse of skyscrapers that might be anywhere that
big money shows itself: New York, a penis-like gherkin in London or
two elephant testicles in Doha. One of them, the intellectual, wears the
Hackers Anonymous mask for a joke but keeps taking it off to show that
it's really him. As the tableau ends, they look up and see Don Q and
Sancho. Individuals from this ensemble will speak, question and
answer, but throughout the scene the rest will become a chorus.*

DON Q
Good evening, all. What might you be celebrating?
*The group looks at the two men and bursts out laughing. A man
approaches him.*
And who may you be?

Don Q (Silvia Weiskopf) and the
Stealth Bankers.

PUBLISHER
A publisher.

DON Q
Do you still produce high-quality books? I only appear in the very
best of them.

PUBLISHER
We still have many good writers.

DON Q
Ah! So you still have a literature.

PUBLISHER
On the contrary, we have a book trade. I like your costume. Be
my guest at the next book fair in Frankfurt.

FEMALE BANKER
Fancy dress? Are you the entertainment we ordered for later? No,
you couldn't be. Our instructions were very specific. No clothes.
You've come to the wrong party, boys.

DON Q
Kind lady, it's an old habit. I've been going to the wrong party all
my life.

SANCHO
This is true . . . Usually it's because he has mistaken a flock of
sheep for ladies of the night.

FEMALE BANKER
He's mistaken me. I'm not a kind lady. I'm a banker in trouble.
Who the hell are you?

CHORUS

Surrounding the two men.

Yes. Who the hell are you?

DON Q

Don Quixote of La Mancha. And this is my loyal and trusted
colleague, Señor Sancho Panza.

FEMALE BANKER

Loyal and trusted colleague? I envy you.

CHORUS

Loyal and trusted colleague? We envy you. Did you see any windmills on the way? Fools. They were wind farms. Were you
attacked by bearded men you thought were priests? Imbeciles.
They were terrorists. Did you assault a policeman because he
looked like the man who stole your purse? Did you? Did you?
Did you? Did you? Well, you were right. He did.

Laughter.

DON Q

We only came to help. Not because you asked for it but because
you need it. Your continent is in ruins. Your people in despair.
The young have no work. You no longer produce what you need
except money.

CHORUS

Miming sadness . . . mocking.

We no longer produce what we need except money. Don Q and
Señor Sancho, you are both very funny. Enlighten us, please.

What should we do to refurbish this old continent and build it
anew? Press the Refresh button on the EU computer?
All on their knees in fake humility.
Don Quixote and Señor Sancho, we will not survive without you.
Tell us what to do. Please tell us what to do.

SANCHO

Is there anyone of authority amongst you?
Half points at the Minister of Finance, half at the Female Banker.
Who makes the decisions?

FINANCE MINISTER

I am the Finance Minister. Without us, the bankers are petrified,
powerless, impotent, incapable of action.

SANCHO

Are you the State?

CHORUS

The State? Who needs the State? Why did you mention the State?
We believe in Freedom, not the State.

DON Q

Taking Sancho to one side.
Enough of this frivolity, Sancho. Spell it out to them, but piano.
Don't lose your temper.

SANCHO

None of you would be here were it not for the State. It creates
you, protects you, bails you out when you're in trouble, will not
replace you even if you can't make anything work. You know all

this, yet you pretend, you falsify the record. You will not even exchange glances with those whose lives you determine because you never encounter them. Perhaps, if they're your parents, you grant them the privilege of seeing you once a year at the time of the winter solstice when our saviour was born. You are far more cruel than any imaginary state. You live in a bubble and when it pops you fall on your knees before the State. Help us please, dear State. The State blows a new bubble for you and you carry on as before.

DON Q

And if I may amplify—

CHORUS

Brutal mimicking.
And if I may amplify. And if I may amplify. And if I may amplify.

DON Q

Enough! Once there were better people than you in our continent. They would see an arid, unpleasant looking piece of land and surround it with walls. They would dig deep, deeper till they found water. They would plant tall palm trees and dates all round, make streams near which they would grow fragrant herbs and build their houses and palaces and soon they had a city which had everything. In the centre, there was a dark mirror in which their glory was reflected. They were so happy that they forgot to look outside. Trouble, when it came, did so from the outside, from a world that the lovers of pleasure had ignored. So they were defeated by the crusade of our Holy Church and those who survived were forced to convert to our faith or expelled from our continent. And so it came about one day that, despite their riches, material and intellectual, they lost everything. Your world is not as refined, but it is not dissimilar. But the way you behave, all I can say is that ignominy awaits you. Yes, Lady Banker and Señor Finance Minister. Ignominy.

The assembly is shaken despite itself but recovers. The two directly named dance a modern quadrille as they undress and caress each other.

FINANCE MINISTER
Quiet. I am the Minister of Financialization.

CHORUS
Oooh, aaaah! Oooh! Aaaah! Pray, silence for the Minister of Financialization. Financialization.

FEMALE BANKER
And I am the producer of finances, without which there would be no financialization.

FINANCE MINISTER
I am the one who makes you, I am the one who decides how long you'll be a banker. How long your fate coincides with your destiny.

FEMALE BANKER
I am the Chairman of the Board. I know the size of the hoard. I know the number of your Zurich account. The names of the women you regularly mount. I know the six diamonds, each as large as a duck's egg, that you were given by the Congo. I've seen

the gifts from Riyadh and Doha, swords made of gold in silver scabbards, watches that would keep a worker's family in comfort for a year. And yet, with all this wealth, you still want to join our board after your rivals are elected to do exactly the same as you. I know, I know, I know.

CHORUS

Knowledge is Power.
Knowledge is Truth.
Knowledge is a cold shower.
Knowledge must be denied to our youth.

FINANCE MINISTER

One phone call, one television interview, the Chairman of the Board will be yesterday's news. Locked in a zoo with other specimens. Dregs of humanity. Soft porn and a diet of decayed vegetable soup. That will be your fate if I decide you're past your sell-by date. You have no choice. Collaborate.

FEMALE BANKER

Enough of recriminations. We're all in this together. We both revel in bribery. We give and we receive. So enough blackmail talk. Enough threats. If I collapse, so will you. We're the scaffolding that holds the system together. We know that in these bad times there are others who make more sacrifices than we do, but we do what we do not just for us but for the future. Yes, a glorious future for our children.

By this stage, they're making love and perhaps children.

Sancho (Jens Ochlast) and Chorus.

CHORUS

If they collapse, so will we all. Our world is fragile and small.
What keeps us strong is that our enemies our weak. They say that
gold is sweet but youth is even sweeter. It's not true any longer.
The youth despair. Their actions are passive. In their despair lies
our hope. Were they to be infected by hope again, who knows
how it would end. Perhaps history would dispatch them to dig
our graves. Best it were not to reach that stage.

INTELLECTUAL

I am the intellectual in their midst.

CHORUS

Bursts out laughing.
The serpent who warms our grass, the dog who licks our arse.

DON Q

What tasks do you really perform?

INTELLECTUAL

I think.
He mimes Rodin pose.
I write.
Reflective pose, hand on face, an imaginary pen.
I speak. I perform important services for our state. I pulverize our
enemies with rhetoric before they meet their fate.

SANCHO

Do you do all this free of charge? Out of the goodness of your
heart?

INTELLECTUAL

Yes.

CHORUS

NO! He works for us. We pay him. We give him honours. Permanent access to television. We need people like him.

INTELLECTUAL

I fight for freedom. I remain a free spirit.

CHORUS

It's true, his spirit is free. We pay for the malt whisky and frozen vodka . . . We need him. He tells the world what we do has to be done and he sounds sincere on television. We don't like his kind. If the world were to change, he would be doing the same for very different people as once he did before.

INTELLECTUAL

Every shift, every new era needs a new language to explain to the people that what is wrong is, in fact, right and what they are experiencing is not destruction but innovation. Not reaction but reform. Not rampant greed, but the spreading of wealth through globalization. And this is how we insert a new language into the consciousness of our citizens. As for those who say I do all this for money, they don't know me well. Power, not money, is the elixir I crave. An evening at the White House, a photograph at the Elysée, a coffee with Muti, a three-minute opportunity with his Holiness at the Vatican. All this is worth more than a million euros because I then am the star. Interviewed everywhere. And when our democracy needs to fight a war, to kill and occupy

another country, who else but I could explain that there are many humanitarian ways to kill humanity?
He smiles without any trace of guilt.

CHORUS

We own the trumpet that he blows. We own the ideas that he spouts. We provide the buzzwords of our new epoch. In these great times, when it is necessary to stifle the lives of people with lies, we need him.

INTELLECTUAL

Señor Sancho, people like you are pitiful. You refuse to accept that this is not one of many fates. It is the only fate. All else has failed. It's true that our capitalism is currently experiencing an unpleasant crisis, but it will pass. All will return to normal and if it doesn't, we will convince the poor that whatever exists is normal.

DON Q

We have known many worlds, heard similar talk, listened to numerous courtiers like yourself. Like you, they have thick knots in their brain that they cannot untie. They have mastered the art of repeating themselves without saying anything. I'm impressed by how practised you are in hiding your servility under the perfect urbanity of manners. Your body language is that of an equal but, suddenly, as a great personage approaches, your mask drops. You become a slave. You are certainly manacled to your fate.
Aside to Sancho.
The new breed that our old Inquisition would have loved.

SANCHO

Your world has collapsed, but you refuse to recognize the fact. It is you who are without an alternative.

FEMALE BANKER

And what is yours? Suppose you were the ruler of the world. What would you do? State control of everything? Genocidal utopias? The plan? Don't make me sick.

SANCHO

Not everything. But everything essential to basic human needs. A poor man sick with a curable disease will die unless he gets a doctor and medicines. What if he can't afford them? What if the queue is far too long? He will die. Physicians can heal themselves. We can't. Your gaze is fixed on the rolling waves of the turbulent ocean. You surf on its successes, you imagine you can override its failures. The great Atlantic Empire-State that has you in its thrall subsidizes what's left of its industry. A world that permanently rewards the rich will not last for ever. You need to change or you will destroy this planet with your greed.

CHORUS

We won't, we won't, we won't. We've heard this rubbish before. Give thanks to our banks. They print and print and print everything that we need. Give thanks to the machines that produce our credit cards. Thanks to holes in high-street walls that vomit out the paper so that we can spend and spend and spend. We may not have the money but we like to think we do. So shove that up your arse, Señor Sancho, and Mr Don Q, too.

DON Q

Look around you. The Parthenon is on fire. The firefighters dispatched by your European Union deliberately forgot to fill their tanks with water. They took petroleum instead. Now the fire spreads. You mocked my colleague Sancho, but let me say this—unless you change, the fire will reach you. The more I look at you, the more I despise you. You are not who you say you are at all. You pretend to be respectable but you're no more than thieves and pimps. That makes you worse. Just a minute. I'm hearing a voice.

Cups his ear and lifts his head.

I hear you. I hear you.

Draws his sword and charges at them. They pretend to fence with him with their knives and forks. The Minister pretends to become a bull and charges him. Don Q is about to pierce him with a sword when Sancho grabs him and disarms him. He gets him a glass of water.

CHORUS

No fat profits? No hedge funds fertilized by your pensions? No easy money for the sharpshooters? He who attacks profits is an intellectual assassin. A terrorist who wishes to destroy our world. To take us back to the dead past. Death to the dead past. Death to the dead past. We have armed men guarding its grave so it can never rise again. As for your scorn, let us tell you, we have endured worse.

SANCHO

Sometimes, one has to go back to move forward.

FINANCE MINISTER

That's what they did in the Middle Ages.

DON Q

Alas, no. They moved forward disastrously. Like you.

SANCHO

If you take the wrong turn and keep walking, you reach a precipice.

FEMALE BANKER

And so? We build a bridge to reach the other side.

SANCHO

How long will that take?

FEMALE BANKER

Who cares? It's the contract to build the bridge that matters.

SANCHO

And what if you actually succeed in building it? You cross and a mile ahead you receive a shock. Something that cannot be bridged. Ever smelt the night air above an abyss?

FEMALE BANKER

Yes, I have. I love life on the edge. I sniff the night air above the abyss. Wonderful. Sensual. It turns me on. What is life without risks?

SANCHO

For you, perhaps. A transition to nowhere. For us, it would be simpler, safer and cheaper to walk back to the main road.

INTELLECTUAL

Too late. We do not believe in Utopia, or a world in which
Utopia is still on the map.

DON Q

Ah. Our rented philosopher.
To Female Banker.
Does your path have a destination?

FEMALE BANKER

We have reached it. Excuse me, I must answer this text. There.
All done. You see . . . in a few seconds I have transferred a few
billion euros from three banks and deposited them in the Bank of
China. Zurich to Beijing. This is the heart of the modern world.
Stay with us. You will learn to love it.

DON Q

What need is there for life? Banks that fail to recognize losses
worth billions of euros on leverages super senior trades are cheat-
ing collateralized debt obligations.

CHORUS

Gasps in shock.
He has penetrated our secret codes. He knows.

*Don Q, pleased with himself, struts around like a rooster on a dung
heap.*

SANCHO

What need is there for the human brain?

FINANCE MINISTER

There are no longer any collective human needs to be fulfilled. Each individual is fulfilled in different ways. That's why we have the same big shops in every big city. The same commodities for sale. Won't you stay with us and learn the new ways?

CHORUS

Stay with us and you will learn that our dictatorship of capital is benign. We permit diversity of every type except political. Our parties are but different brands of the same product. Each offers the same diet and those who refuse to partake will go hungry. Those who think liberty cannot be bought for money are unaware that money is liberty. We are teaching our people that there is no past and no future. Only the present. Live in it, shop in it, fuck in it, steal in it, swim in it, die in it. They taught us once that death is the great leveller. It comes for the rich and the poor, in the mansion house and the hovel, but ask yourselves this—who dies happier?

DON Q

Let go of me, Sancho. I can't take this any more. Listen to their complacent conceit. I will drive them out. I will drive them out! Come, Sancho.

Both men draw their swords and charge again, creating mayhem. Crockery is being broken. This time, the whole party is a bit frightened and they run off the stage. Don Q raises his sword with his arm out-stretched and looks up at the sky. A halo lights his face.

DON Q

I have driven the money-men out of the temple, O Lord.

Lights out. The stage is empty except for Don Q and Sancho, who are fast asleep as the dimmer lights return.

Rocinante and Mule stand up waiting for their masters.

VOICE OF DON Q

Loud and angry.

Sancho, Sancho. Wake up. We must save the world from itself. Sancho, did you hear me? Never bring me water again. Something stronger. Milk. I want milk. Sancho, milk. Sancho, milk.

ROCINANTE

I think they had a very bad dream. I heard the master talk in his sleep. Sorry I interrupted you. What did you say?

MULE

Who created us?

ROCINANTE

What kind of dumb question is that? The great master Cervantes, of course. Who else?

MULE

God.

ROCINANTE

Listen, you obstinate fool. We're animals. We don't have to believe in God. That's meant for the superior species.

MULE

Why did Cervantes create us?

ROCINANTE

Because he was a genius. I think he made me a bit like himself.
But those who ride us were not so lucky.

MULE

To hear them talk about love, I'm glad it doesn't exist for us. Was
our creator a Christian?

ROCINANTE

Yes, but his grandparents and their parents were Jews. And he
insisted that the person who really invented us was a Moor, a
Muslim.
Laughs.

MULE

Bad enough to be created by a descendant of Jews, but for Cer-
vantes to create a double fiction that a Muslim wrote our history.
Too much. Too bloody much.
Crosses himself.
God preserve us from Jews and Muslims.

ROCINANTE

Inquisition talk. You can't say these things now, at least not about
the Jews.

*Music. Don Q and Sancho wake up and are startled by a woman run-
ning onto the stage. She dominates all. Rocinante and Mule run away
in fear. A dance of death. She is on fire.*

As they ride off, the scene shifts to an unfashionable bar. It's empty. The
bartender, a woman in her twenties, ears plugged to music, punkish
hair, sulky manner, is reading Sartre's Critique of Dialectical Reason. *Sancho and Don Q are hidden in partial darkness, drinking beer*
and eating bread and cheese.
Man walks in. In his sixties, long grey hair. Wearing jeans and a
moth-eaten thick sweater.

MAN
A large whisky. Table for two?

She smiles ironically, gesturing to empty tables, follows him as he selects
one and lights a candle in an empty wine bottle. She brings a whisky.

MAN
A great misfortune happened to me here two months ago. She
did not arrive. My heart missed a few beats. This annoyed me
more than her not showing up. I suppose it's the way I'm made.
Happy moments are soon forgotten. A sorrowful hour? Never.
How times change. Once, a married woman would have been
pleased by the thought that a man loved her, but she would not
have considered a physical compact unless she was prepared to
leave her husband. *Anna Karenina?* A tabloid novel. Intellectually,
it might have been more pleasing if Anna had been married to

Vronsky and had an affair with Karenin. Then Vronsky could
have thrown himself in front of a train. A play along those lines,
that reverses the plot of the original, might work.
Chuckles to himself.
Then we had women becoming more forward and thinking to
themselves: Hmm. I mustn't love him because I'm married, but
he's madly in love with me and so . . . As for now, just wait and
see. That's if she turns up.

*Enter Woman. Dark-haired, in her early fifties, elegantly attired,
bespectacled. He gives her a polite smile and they exchange a perfunc-
tory kiss. Then his mood changes. His eyes light up and he drags her
close to him and kisses her on the lips. Her arms remain by her side. She
does not respond. Her indifference is obvious. His arms drop, his eyes
fade. He is resigned but sad. Bartender, still reading her book, walks to
the table and puts a whisky in front of her.*

WOMAN
Well?

MAN
You're late again.

WOMAN
I'm here.

MAN
Unlike two months ago.

WOMAN
Unlike two months ago. Had you bought a cellphone as I advised
you, I could have texted you.

MAN

I don't know why I don't believe you.

She laughs.

WOMAN

What grows, yet becomes less?

MAN

Have you decided what we're going to do?

WOMAN

Have you noticed that since we were last here that girl has got
through half of that Sartre volume? It gives one hope.

MAN

I wish you would give me some hope.

WOMAN

Why did you give me that frozen smile when I walked in? A dry,
dead smile. Was it to improve the vacant look on your face? I pre-
ferred you before you fell in love with me. You were lively, funny,
alert, engaged. Now you moan non-stop like a cow in labour.

MAN

Vacant? No. Tormented. Should I leave? I won't leave alone. In
my memory, stored for ever—your words, your laugh, your gestures. Stored for ever.

WOMAN

Gets up.

My husband's taken a young whore. I'm left with a morose old
bore. I need a piss.

Man (Sven Seeburg), Don Q (Silvia Weiskopf), Sancho (Jens Ochlast) and Bartender.

MAN
Aside.

Even the drops of her piss will echo with harsh sounds. Two sum-
mers ago. First I saw her back, tanned and glistening in the sun.
Her hair flying in the breeze. Not like now. She's had it cut. Bru-
talism on every front. She was watching the sea and as I passed
her to swim, I avoided looking at her face . . . or her breasts. A
dual sacrifice. She was still there when I returned an hour later.
Sitting on the sand . . . she smiled and . . .

Woman returns.

WOMAN
I hate Chopin's Polonaise.

MAN
It's the first positive thing you've said for many months.
*Woman suppresses a laugh, makes a note in her diary. Man turns in
the direction of Don Q and Sancho.*
Sad, shy, dreamy? Don't be deceived. Pale, contemplative, intense
and very strange. In her youth she never hid her true feelings.
Defied convention and her parents, shocked her friends, isolated
herself from society. And now?
Turns to her.
Let's talk about you. About family life. Your four sons, your
husband.

WOMAN

Your wife, your twins, the toilet paper on which you write your books. Why you always choose this fucking place and why you get on my nerves so much. Get an analyst.

MAN

Look, those two guys are coming over. Amazing gear. Like a painting I once saw of Don Quixote and Sancho Panza. Do you think they're actors?

WOMAN

I have to go.

DON Q

Please don't. We couldn't help overhearing your conversation.

MAN

I'm sorry. We must seem very strange to you.

SANCHO

A man in love but a woman taking her time. It's universal.

WOMAN

He's taking my time! My mind is clear.

DON Q

Ah, well observed, Sancho. But love, dear friends, is like a veg-etable market. Unless you take advantage of its freshness, it rots. And in your case I fear . . .

Don Q (Silvia Weiskopf), Woman (Ines Krug), Man (Sven Seeburg) and Bartender.

WOMAN

Do you think just because we're of a certain age, you can make
these stupid . . .

DON Q

Madame, forgive me. I was referring to your gentleman friend.
Your beauty is, of course, ageless. Your clarity admirable. Your
mind profound, but a word of advice. Either go with him or do
what must be done and put him out of his misery. Don't make
him suffer too much.

WOMAN

But he's like you. He likes suffering. He thinks I'm Dulcinea.
Emotionally crippled by his own stunted imagination. A bit of
Adorno might still do him some good. Your company will only
make the disease incurable. You, Don Quixote, are a physician
who must first cure himself.

DON Q

Madame, I have. What you refer to was part of my first adventures. I have learnt many lessons since then, which is why I am so
bold as to offer you some disinterested advice.

WOMAN

I can do without it. I'm off. I won't be back. In a year's time, perhaps, we can meet for a coffee and laugh at the fact that you were
ever like this . . .

MAN

What she will never understand is that ice can set hearts on fire.
Follies often lead to heroic passions.

WOMAN

Heroic passions are always a folly. They never last. The heroism
goes very soon. The passion follows.

MAN

For you, perhaps. Just look at you. No energy at all. Drained of
everything. Passion. Ideas. Everything.

WOMAN

I think I was happiest when my virginity was intact. A lot of
admirers, but no action. And then my husband happened. And
then children and now you. Why can't you forget your fucking
passion? I offered you a light-hearted friendship. You said yes but
you meant no.

MAN

I can't fuck a light-hearted friendship.

WOMAN

Then go fuck yourself.
She glares at all of them and walks briskly offstage.

DON Q

A remarkable lady.

SANCHO

If my Teresa behaved like that I'd slap her.

MAN

She's left me. She must have found someone else. Someone
younger, more alert to her many needs. Could it be . . . could it
be . . . might she have become a lesbian? Her haircut suggests . . .

Bartender walks over to the three men.

BARTENDER

Whenever a woman leaves a guy must there be someone else,
male or female? Pathetic. Never heard of contingent love and
necessary love?

ALL THREE MEN TOGETHER

Contingent? Necessary? Love? No. What is this monster. Aren't
you too young to know?

BARTENDER

She mimes to music as she speaks.

Once upon a time in the city of light, there lived a couple who
never did fight. They loved. They drank. They talked. They were
close friends. They were Jean-Paul and Simone. They wrote and
wrote till their minds remained alert. The bad coffee must have
helped. He wrote this great work and many others. She wrote
and taught us women not to be dutiful. No. Not to Father or
Husband or Mother or Priest. But to the World, to Truth, to
Love. But what is love? It can be contingent, short-term, an acci-
dent, you get it over with. Or it can be necessary, because intellectual affinities are infinities. They outlive physical passions. Well.
That's all. Now do you understand?

DON Q

What a vulgar idea. Did it work?

SANCHO

A bad excuse for non-stop adultery.

MAN

Did any good come of it at last?

BARTENDER

Even the best principles in the world are difficult to implement. It was not easy. She fell in love with another. Was it contingent or necessary? Or both? He was rough. He was tender. He taught her what the *Critique of Dialectical Reason* never discussed. The benefits of an orgasm and how it happens. She had her first taste of this new delight, but it was not enough. She refused to commit herself to the Orgasm Man. It drove him crazy. You whore, he said. You used my body and now you're going back to that squint-eyed monster who reminds me of a travelling shoe salesman. She wept. He froze. She returned to Jean-Paul. He carried on writing.

ALL THREE MEN TOGETHER

They must have read Adorno. Yes. They must have read Adorno. They must have.

BARTENDER

Let me put it clearly. The idea's simple. If I want to shag someone I fancy, I just do it. No need to make it sound more important than it is . . . but a few months ago, I met a guy. A bit older than me. In his early fifties, and he made me laugh and I wanted more than just a shag so I thought I'd go and read a few books. And do you know something? They've become like aphrodisiacs. The shagging's acquired more depth, if you'll pardon the expression.

DON Q

Your profundity has stirred something in me once again.

SANCHO

Oh no. God protect us.

Don Q stands up. He leaps and jumps around her. Sancho calms him down and takes him away.

MULE

I know I've not read as much as you, Rocinante. But I do consider myself cultivated. Sartre and Brecht I understand. The first a gifted philosopher, the second a much greater artist, hated by the banker's world. But Adorno? Should I have heard of him?

ROCINANTE

You should be ashamed of yourself. Mule, I fear my lust for you might be contingent and not necessary unless you read Adorno. His short reflections on life and art, his aphorisms, his letters . . . All these are without compare. He is one of a kind. What the superior species were referring to was a few sentences from 'Post Festum', a reflection on erotic love. Listen carefully: 'Pain at the decay of erotic relationships is not just, as it takes itself to be, fear of love's withdrawal, nor the kind of narcissistic melancholy that has been penetratingly described by Freud. Also involved is fear of the transience of one's own feeling.'

MULE

Brilliant. It's exactly how I feel after I've fucked you.

Rocinante (Ingrid Domann)
and Mule (Jan Pröhl).

Angel of History is lowered onto the stage backwards. She is in a silver body stocking. She flaps her wings.

ANGEL OF HISTORY
Stop this play immediately. Now!

DON Q
Who is this delicious creature?

ANGEL OF HISTORY
I am the Angel of History.

DON Q
She who must be obeyed. At your service, dearest Angel.

ANGEL OF HISTORY
Every member of the cast onstage, please listen to the great reprimand.

Cast, extras, designers pack the stage.

ANGEL OF HISTORY
And the director and author?
Roci and Mule walk to her and bow.
You are the director and author. I should have guessed!

ROCINANTE/MULE

Yes you should have. You prefer to serve Heaven. We prefer to reign in Hell. All the good people are with us.

ANGEL OF HISTORY

What you are doing is not Cervantes!

ROCINANTE

How could it be? But he would have liked it.

MULE

We can say things now that he could only think.

ROCINANTE

Don Quixote appears delusional, but it is just an act he puts on to deceive the Church and the Holy Brotherhood. You don't know them. Europe's first secret police, fighting the war on intellectual terror.

ANGEL OF HISTORY

Cervantes completed his novel. Your structure is . . . is . . . er . . . is . . .

MULE

Excuse me, Angel of History, our times are different but the structure is very loyal to the great master of Alcalá. Scenes big and scenes small and candlelight to read the writing on the wall.

ROCINANTE

Travels that never end. New dangers around every bend. Some things change. Others remain the same. The echoes of time past

never disappear. But you must know that, Angel of History. Stay
and watch what else we have in store.

ANGEL OF HISTORY

Thank you, but I must return to reassure Cervantes and my special friend, Walter Benjamin, that you mean well. I might become
invisible tomorrow and join the audience.

ALL ONSTAGE

Farewell and welcome. Fly carefully. Avoid the furies of our
planet where fires burn and filth pollutes the air.

ROCINANTE/MULE

Enough distractions for one play. Come on. Get on with it. The
play continues.

*Dark stage. War music. Noises of jets. Drones. Whirring helicopters.
Explosions.*

Mule (Jan Pröhl).

Sancho (Jens Ochlast), Poet (Rezo Tschchikwischwili) and Don Q (Silvia Weiskopf).

ACT II

Don Q and Sancho ride into an empty space, a deserted highway in Germany with road signs. A big one points to LANDSTUHL MILI-TARY HOSPITAL. On the side a dark-skinned beggar is sitting on the ground playing a flute, a lament for a lost past. There is an empty plate in front of him. Enchanted by the music, the two men dismount.

SANCHO
Whispers.
Another Roma?

DON Q
Perhaps. Have you a coin?
The two men dismount, walk on tiptoes to the beggar and are about to lay a coin gently on the plate when the beggar stops playing and looks at them.

We apologize. It was not our intention to disturb you. To distract
you from your music. It seems to come straight from your
wounded heart. I am Don Quixote and this is my friend Sancho
Panza.

POET

You were created such a long time ago. So nice to see you in the
flesh. So refreshing. Such a relief from this suffering world.

SANCHO

Are you a musician?

POET

A poet. Doomed to exile with my begging bowl. Far, far away
from where I was born—in the heart of Baghdad.

SANCHO

Family?

POET

A bitter laugh escapes.

Family? They died a million deaths. They left five million orphans
behind. And I, a poet, neither Sunni nor Shia, sing for them every
day. My verse is no longer heard. My imagination is drowned in
blood. I inhaled the uranium from their shells and bombs and
now I fear it might emerge in liquid form and blind me. So I dare
not weep. My wife was gang-raped in prison. I saw the photograph the perpetrators sent back home. Six penises tattooed with
stars and stripes, one with the union jack. The prison warders
who watched were wearing blue waistcoats with stars. Not a day

goes by that I don't think of her. She was my wife, my country, my life. The music I make are the tears that flow each day. This continent in which you travel, your ancestral home and now my refuge, is in pain. Its memory gone, it lives only in the present, enjoying its machines, big and small. Thank you for stopping.

Lifts his flute and begins to play once again, oblivious to all else. Suddenly, Poet's cell phone rings. He speaks in Arabic. The two men watch and then hurriedly walk away.

DON Q

We used to say: The country that controls the sea controls the world.

SANCHO

Now it's the space above us. Whoever controls that space can destroy the world.

POET

Shouts.

Come back, come back. My friend was ringing to warn that a gang is coming to attack me. They've been trying to get me for months. I'm always one step ahead of them. Let's run before they get here.

Even as they help him collect his things, a purple darkness envelops the stage and some hooded figures, some tattooed hoodlums have surrounded them. Each speaks and the others act as chorus.

TATTOOED MAN

Who are you?

POET

A human being.

CHORUS

A human being. No. You're a sick joke. Answer before you die. Are you asylum seeker, immigrant, Muslim, refugee or Roma?

SANCHO

He is our friend. We are travelling musicians.

TATTOOED MAN

Who asked you to speak, arsehole?

CHORUS

Speak when you're spoken to or we will cut out your tongue. Now answer in turn. Who are you?

TATTOOED MAN

To Poet.

First you.

POET

I am a poet from Baghdad, living here in exile. Your police is aware of me. They have a big file.

DON Q

Aside.

Suddenly it's clear what needs to be done. This brotherhood is not holy. It worships the sun, it burns, it kills, it destroys, it feeds on depression and despair, it offers a way out that leads directly to Hell.

To Poet.

Sancho and I will hold them back as only we can. You run while we stay. Inform the authorities. Send help. You must live. Never forget your songs are important. Never. Now go. Sancho, remember that these are no windmills. They will fight back. So when I give the signal, unsheath your sword, cock your pistol and let flashing fire follow. First I will try to reason with them so that our Arab friend has more time to get out of this hell.

To racists.

Gentlemen, could I suggest a short round-table conference. After all we are all rational people. There is no need for violence of this sort. You sir, with that beautiful tattoo on your head. Why not sit down and talk. You know that in olden times there were people who behaved like this but realized that such methods were disastrous. So let us speak.

Gang laughs, whisper to one another. Their tattooed leader comes to Don Q and they shake hands.

GANG LEADER

We shall listen to your words of wisdom and then decide our future course of action. It is not often that we have the chance to meet people like you. Let's hope it doesn't rain.

DON Q

You are a consummate diplomat, sir. You will go far. Who knows, perhaps one day a future president or prime minister. You have sowed enough wild oats. Time to abandon your delusions.

All sit down on the stage in a circle. We see them as if from a distance.
Don Q miming a reasonable speech. The gang nod and listen, all the
time winking at one another. Then the gang stands up and simulates
pissing on the head of Don Q and Sancho. The two men, swords
unsheathed and pistols drawn, move forward. The gangsters cannot
believe what they are witnessing. They laugh. They mock. They bare
their backsides and they pretend to run away till Don Q fires a pistol
and one of them screams and drops. Then the gang, angered by this,
turn round and a choreographed battle commences to the music of flute
and drum. After some minutes in which swords are raised, Tattooed
Man takes out a dagger and stabs Don Q in the arm. He falls. Sancho
is surrounded by a menacing circle and kicked till unconscious. The
sound of police cars and ambulances. The gangsters run offstage.
Ambulance men arrive, put the two fallen men on stretchers and, to
the noise of sirens, take them away. Stage changes colours. It's now
bright again.

Enter Rocinante and Mule.

MULE

Where did they take them? I heard one of them saying Landstuhl
was the nearest hospital for an emergency.

ROCINANTE

Landstuhl? Oh, yes. A large US military hospital. Very good doc-
tors. They'll be fine. Oh no. Hope they've got insurance. They
can pretend they're soldiers. Soldiers of fortune.

MULE

Even though Sancho sometimes whips me, I don't like seeing
them beaten up.

ROCINANTE

I'm glad we were not present. Those gangsters looked unpleasant.
If they had found out that both your master and mine were not
created by an old Christian they might have killed us all.

MULE

My master is an old Christian. It makes me proud of him.

ROCINANTE

So is my master, you fool. I'm talking about our über-Master
who created us all, and please don't say God again.

MULE

Oh, Cervantes. Hmm. Who cares? Not me. Anyway, he's dead. We're still here. Roci, did you hear that poet describe how his wife was raped by six men? And your master muttered under his breath, 'The animals, the animals.'

ROCINANTE

I was not pleased at all. In fact, only humans behave like that . . .

MULE

Because they're the superior species?

ROCINANTE

And every act they can't explain they blame on us. Did we send the Jews to the gas chamber?

MULE

Did we nuke Hiroshima and Nagasaki?

ROCINANTE

Or bomb Dresden? Or drop chemicals on Vietnam? Or use depleted uranium shells in Iraq? I can't deny that we sometimes do stupid things like leaping off the edge and committing collective suicide . . .

MULE

But that's very different from collective murder.

ROCINANTE

I suppose we'd better go to the forest, spend the night there and then tomorrow morning make our way to Landstuhl.

MULE

Do you think they're still alive? I only asked.

Exit lights dim. Night. Scene moves to ward in US military hospital in Landstuhl.
Nurses checking on patients. Don Q and Sancho's clothes are hanging beside their beds. Sancho has intravenous tubes. Don Q is wide awake. Others are asleep.

Hospital noises. Sounds of wounded soldiers talking in their sleep. The odd scream. Nurse rushes to the bed. Tranquilizes the soldier. Silence returns. Don Q, in a white hospital gown and helmet, gets out of bed and first inspects the ward, makes sure Sancho is sleeping and then tiptoes to face the audience. When required, Don Q gestures and a ghost-like soldier will be spotlighted as s/he gets out of bed to come forward and speak.

DON Q

Aside. Soft voice, almost a whisper.

They talk to each other of the splendid scenery in Afghanistan. The snow-capped peaks. The inaccessible crags. The treacherous streams almost as bad as the people. Afghans, or hajis as they call them. They speak of villages on the edge of nowhere where everyone they were told was a friend turned out to be an enemy. So they killed, not knowing whom they were killing and not caring either. Private X. Come here please.

Private X gets out of his bed as if he were a ghost. His head is bandaged. His face disfigured.

PRIVATE X

Salutes.

Private X. Rodrigues, sir.

DON Q

Please repeat what you told me earlier.

PRIVATE X

My mother didn't want me to come here. She tried her best to
stop me, but the Marine Corps promised that if I stayed for two
years they would pay my college fees and medical insurance. I
stayed six years. Señor Quixote, when I first came I loved life
intensely. I did not want to tear lives to shreds. I did not want to
strip anybody naked. I was no different from the people in
Afghanistan. Our military was aware of the problem. They deraci-
nated the enemy. The haj. Hajis. Muslims. Terrorists. It was OK
to kill them. They were not just the enemy. They were not like us.
Not even their children. My senior officer told me: 'Don't be
taken in by their innocent smiles. Underneath the smile there is a
bomb. Children in these countries are sometimes more dangerous
than adults.' I couldn't believe what I was hearing till I saw an
eleven-year-old boy hurl a grenade at one of my buddies and kill
him. I shot the kid dead. Just like that . . . pumped ten bullets
into him. Three weeks later, I fell in love with an Afghan girl.

Flashback scene within the scene.

We were under attack. I found myself in a small hut. I had
fainted. I saw her when I opened my eyes. It was love at first
sight. We met many times and then . . .

AFGHAN GIRL

Wearing a hijab and covering herself with a cheap blanket, stroking his head on her lap.

Marine boy, I know you love me, but to marry me you must become a Muslim first. Come and meet my family. They know about you.

Stage goes dark. We see them in silhouettes as if through night-vision goggles. She takes him by the hand and they walk in circles. It's a trap. She runs away. Sounds of bullets and shouts of 'kill the infidel'.

PRIVATE X

I grabbed her sister as a shield. The bullets still came. I slit the sister's throat, hid behind the TV and as her father and brothers came I blew the fuckers to eternity. They shouldn't fuck with Marines. And then . . .

He fires at the Afghan girl. End of flashback.

That night I got the shivers. They injected me with Valium. A few months later I learnt to inject myself with something better. I killed other kids too. Revenge is simply their everyday life. What else can they do? And they got me. I wish I'd killed more of the fuckers. Perhaps I will when I get home. If I see a towel-head motherfucker in Tallahassee, God help him.

He walks back slowly to the bed.

DON Q

How will these soldiers be normal again? Storms of misfortune await them. As for those they have left behind in a country afflicted by a Thirty-Year War, where the yellow moon in summer lights up the blood embedded in rocks and the earth. Oh cruel, passive all-knowing God who watches all this, century after century, as people kill in his name. Nothing changes.

Unknown to him, a woman soldier has hobbled up to Don Q. She taps him on the shoulder. He jumps. Unbeknown to them both Sancho has quietly got out of bed with his tubes still fixed to his nose and is watching Don Q.

SOLDIER-WOMAN

Who are you?

DON Q

Aside.

She's lovely. My heart, my broken heart. My anguished heart, what should I do? Should I break my foolish vows of chastity to her? She who never appears. Does she even exist outside my tortured imagination?

Turns to the woman.

Don Quixote at your service, madame.

SOLDIER-WOMAN

Don Quixote! Cool. From La Mancha, I presume. Of course. Where else. Long way from La Mancha to Landstuhl. And look at you. My God, you're so slim. So chic. So modern. Are you on a special diet? How do you manage to keep so trim? Look at me.

Lifts her gown to reveal her stomach. Don Q takes a deep breath and looks away, embarrassed.

Want to share a joint?

DON Q

We have not been introduced.

SOLDIER-WOMAN

Sorry. I am Major Dulcinea Rodamonte, a medical officer with
the US Marines. I was wounded and discharged, almost at the
same time. I return to Miami tomorrow.

DON Q

In a daze since he heard the magic name. He speaks with love in his
eyes. She's delighted with such an easy conquest.
Dulcinea, Dulcinea. Who could hurt you?

SOLDIER-WOMAN

Let's call it friendly fire. A risk of the trade. Not a nice story, Don
Q. Sure you want to hear it?
She mimes as she speaks. Music.
A senior officer walked into my office. I knew him officially.
Always thought he was a decent guy. He often stared at my
breasts, but what the hell. I didn't think too much of it. There are
hundreds of brothels in Afghanistan, with tarts of every type,
ready to serve these motherfuckers. Give them what they want as
long as they pay in dollars or euros. There are 15 other NATO
currencies but these gals won't take them. This sonofabitch walks
in. At first he says nothing. I see the gleam of lust in his eyes. 'I'd
like to fuck you, Dulcie,' he tells me. My revolver is lying in front
of me. I lift it. 'You try that and I'll blow your balls off, General
or no General.' The thought excites him and he opens his flies
and puts his filthy prick on my desk. Then he grabs me. I point
my revolver at his balls. He tried to snatch it from me and the

weapon went off by mistake. His balls survived to rape another day. My foot was badly damaged. I told my boss what happened. He advised me not to take it further or I'd lose my privileges. I was a coward. Honourably discharged. He was transferred to Fort Bragg. Don't look so upset, Don. It was my fault. I should have stayed a civilian. Hey, I love the cut of your beard. Reminds me of a young Afghan doctor I once knew. We were both students in Baltimore. You're a very attractive man, Don Quixote.

DON Q

Madame, I am no doctor, but I have studied the living chords of the human heart all my life. You have my deepest sympathy.

She begins to caress his face. At first, Don Q is startled, but soon he begins to like it. Still in dream mode, all he can mutter is 'Dulcinea . . . Dulcinea' as they dance. As the petting reaches a new stage, he is squirming with delight.

SOLDIER-WOMAN

O my man, O my man, take me to your bed. I will press your feet, kiss your lips, massage your head, rub oil on your groin and, when all sounds disappear and nothing can be heard, I promise I'll comb your beard. My heart leaps like a fish in water.

Sancho steps forward. She laughs. Don Q is ashamed.

SANCHO

Forgive, me madame, I think your name has had a magical effect on my friend here. Please take care, because his age is not what it seems and what once rose to the sky like a red-hot flame is now buried in ice. All physical contact is torment for him. If you insist

on completing your rape—forgive me, I mean your seduction—
he might lose his life.

*She glares at Sancho and clings to Don Q. Lights go on and all the
other patients, wide awake, become the chorus, punctuated by solo
voices.*

CHORUS
(THE SONG OF THE WOUNDED SOLDIERS)
We all know what rape is
We all know what we have to do
When we're taught to rape a country
It means its people too;
We're led by a dog called Satan
We answer only to his call
If we try and resist his orders
All our heads will fall.

SOLO WOMAN
Who wants to die in a foreign land
Far away from our languages and our songs
Homesick for our children, homesick for Burger Kings
Homesick for our people
I only wish that I had wings. Please don't get me wrong.
Our hardworking, trusting, poor people
Each trying to earn a crust.
Not working because there ain't no work
Living off handouts to eat what makes us fat, fatter, each passing
year
And so we die before our time.

Soldier-Woman (Ines Krug) and
Don Q (Silvia Weiskopf).

CHORUS

Kabul the city, Kabul the river
Cursed the country, we tried to deliver.
First the English came with sword, lance and bugle,
A century later the Russians with Kalashnikovs
And now it's us—US, NATO, ISAF,
Forty-eight countries in a mess.
Three generations of Afghans embedded in wars. Turquoise twi-
lights, the delights of the bazaar,
And all the while
Death observes you from the hill.

SOLO MAN

We make the law for others, never for ourselves.
Those who enforce the law are not obliged to obey it.
We make the law to punish our enemies and sometimes those
who forget that they are our friends.
Given that this is the case, there can never be any question of us
having committed an offence under any law.
We all know what rape is.

CHORUS

We all know what we have to do
When we're taught to rape a country
It means its people too;
We're led by a dog called Satan
We answer only to his call
If we try and resist his orders
All our heads will fall.

Enter Nurse, who shouts.

NURSE

What is this noise! Will you please be quiet? This is not the time for noise. Go to sleep. Tomorrow, there will be a last inspection. You will be dressed properly. Very important people are coming to see you and after that you will be airmailed home.

Lights dim. Don Q and Soldier-Woman are in a bed together. She is under the blanket.

SOLDIER-WOMAN
Whispers.
Comfortable now, my Don . . . just let me move so we're both comfortable. Sancho was so wrong. Make love to me. Nothing predictable. Like rhymeless verses with irregular rhythms.

A love groan from Don Q.

NURSE
Screams.
Quiet!!!

Silence. Lights out. Music. Sunrise. A forest glade. Birdsong.

Don Q (Silvia Weiskopf) and
Soldier-Woman (Ines Krug).

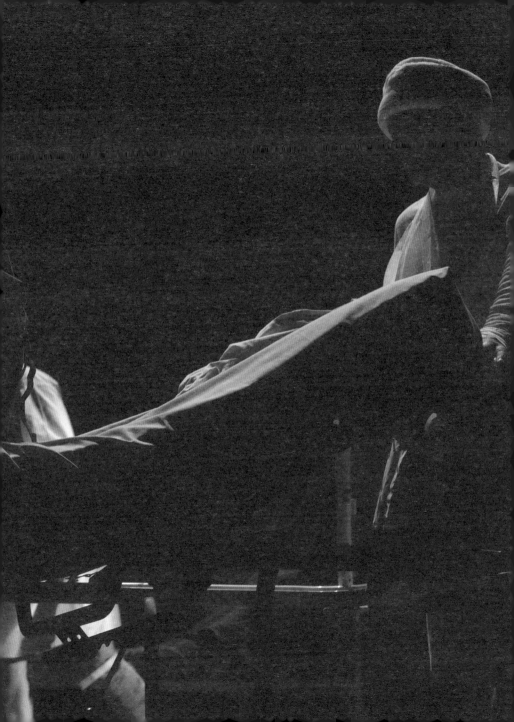

Rocinante is reading Montaigne. Mule is just waking up.

MULE

I'm hungry. I wish there was a farm near here where we could steal some oats. What are you reading? Ah, Montaigne. What a poseur . . . I mean you, not Montaigne. He was a clever geezer.

ROCINANTE

Cicero says somewhere that the study of philosophy is designed simply to make us learn how to die.

MULE

That is either very profound or very banal. I'm not sure which . . .

ROCINANTE

You never will be . . .

MULE

All I can tell you is that your master was not learning how to die in that hospital, but how to live.

ROCINANTE

Are you sure? What do you mean?

Mule does a vulgar little mime whose meaning is unmistakeable.

I see. Oh well, I'm pleased. Contingent lust is always a better cure than necessary lust. Are we picking them up today?

MULE

In the afternoon all the invalids will be discharged, but there is some big farewell event with politicians and celebrities and photo-calls for the media.

Both animals lift their hind legs and fart in unison.

ROCINANTE/MULE

I'm glad we're in agreement.

MULE

Rocinante, one thing has been worrying me. You know that book you were reading aloud to me last night? You know the one.

ROCINANTE

Of course. Marx's manifesto.

MULE

Are Marx's laws valid only for classes or also for individuals?

ROCINANTE

I'm not sure I understand you.

MULE

I mean, can there be a good individual bourgeois and a bad individual worker?

ROCINANTE

Yes, of course. And many bad bourgeois and many bad workers.

MULE

What category do our masters fall into?

ROCINANTE

Hmm. Let me think. Neither of them is attached to the means of production. They own very little property, so categorizing them as peasant proprietors would be slightly inaccurate.

MULE

But he is DON Quixote.

ROCINANTE

A mask to deceive the enemy. I suppose they are déclassé elements constantly confronting contradictory class locations. They could become frenzied petty bourgeois, but that is unlikely. Though I'm not sure of Sancho Panza. He can sometimes behave like a lumpen nationalist.

MULE

Like Joan of Arc?

ROCINANTE

The analogy is not without humour, but imprecise.

MULE

The sun shines. To Landstuhl, where our masters await.

Fake cheerful music, perhaps the Radetsky March, as the scene shifts back to the hospital ward which now looks very different. It is totally clean. All the patients look very neat but covered with sheets, including Sancho and Don Q.

Rocinante (Ingrid Domann).

*Choreographed scene. Fake cheerful music stops as cameras enter, ready
to film the event. Then, on cue, a uniformed General weighed down
with medals, a senior politician wearing an EU-flag jacket and an
obvious celebrity wearing a low-cut dress enter, and cameras flash. The
trio move to a bed where a very pretty young soldier is sitting up. She's
asked by the cameraman to stand up and pose for a photograph with
the visitors. Nurses rush to help her as she gets out because she has neither arms nor legs. She flashes a smile. The trio and the cameraman
freeze in horror. Suddenly, all the other invalids get up and stand in
front of their beds with crutches, bandaged foreheads and single arms
and glare at the intruders. Then they make a circle round them like a
dance of death. Slight panic as the trio rush to a spot where there is a
semblance of 'normalcy'—the beds in front of which Don Q and Sancho
are standing in their uniforms, with helmets and swords. The trio
shake hands with them and pose for photographs. Flashes. Filming.
Then Don Q and Sancho suddenly turn their backs on the visitors, pull
down their trousers and show them their naked behinds. The visitors
and cameras freeze. They are hurriedly ushered to the edge of the ward.
As they move to the side, an eruption of spontaneous laughter as everyone kisses and hugs each other. Music and a dance of life, which ends
with the woman without arms and legs being lifted and placed on a*

throne-like high chair and greeted like a goddess. They all assemble on
either side of her.

CHORUS

First 14 lines are sung looking at the trio and their media. The rest at
the audience.

You, who send us to fight your wars
Understand that life is no laughing matter.
We kill and we die
And there is no such thing as killing
Or dying in a humanitarian way.
All wars just and unjust
Are wars. And today, as oil fuels religion
What is just to your side is unjust to the other.
You, who want people to love you
Make them your enemy if they refuse; and they have reasons why
they do,
Ask this of us?
And if we reply: No, we do not love you
Will you declare us to be the enemy?
And you who stay at home
You sleepwalkers who dream yourselves out of trouble
So that there is no need any more to think.
One day you will have to wake up.
Understand that life is no laughing matter.
Life is no laughing matter.

Enter Rocinante and Mule. Their masters mount them, ready to leave.

SANCHO

We leave you now to visit the Holy Lands. The Via Dolorosa is
certainly no laughing matter. We shall think of you in the desert,
the site of all temptations. Do not worry. We will resist them.

CHORUS

Farewell to our kind friends from nowhere and everywhere. Safe
journey to the desert where you go. We return to lands where
truth is ridiculed and those who spread it are put behind bars. We
carry the truth on our misshapen bodies and it gets heavier by the
day. But you be careful.

If you bare your behinds in desert climes, the aroused
masses might devour your arses. Or kick your butt so that it is
for ever shut.

Repeat last sentence.

They wave an exaggerated farewell. Music. Don Q and Sancho exit.

The media re-enters with cameras, etc. They are accompanied by a
strange man dressed in tails who walks and speaks very slowly.

NOBEL-COMMITTEE MAN
Is one of you Private X?

Spotlight on Private X.

PRIVATE X
That's me.

NOBEL-COMMITTEE MAN
I come on behalf of the Nobel Peace Prize Committee.

PRIVATE X
I think you've got the wrong man. Surely you want Don
Quixote?

NOBEL-COMMITTEE MAN
Certainly not. He's never killed anyone. This prize is awarded
only to those who help peace by making war. It's a lot of money.
Millions of dollars.

PRIVATE X
Smiles.
Just for killing children? Or adults as well?

NOBEL-COMMITTEE MAN

For preserving the peace.

PRIVATE X

Let me consult my colleagues.

The wounded get together and mime a debate/discussion, each whispering in another's ear. Then they surround the Nobel-Committee Man.

CHORUS

We may be poor, we may have a price,
But the dynamite you offer is not very nice.
Bashing skulls and bombing weddings are things we will never
forget.
We know what peace is and we know it's not what we do.
So take your filthy money and give it to rascals who think like
you.

TV cameras, photographers crowd around Private X, waiting for his decision.

PRIVATE X

Hey, all of you, cut out the shit. This guy's right, man. Our Generals decide who lives, who dies. We obey orders, but we do so to maintain the peace. We kick their balls, we kick their guts, we destroy all feeling in our hearts to rip these terrorists apart. We smash their skulls, we bomb their weddings, we dynamite their funerals. That's us. Don't ever fuck with a Marine. We make war because we love peace. Thank you, Mr Nobel Prize Man. What fun. I accept your prize that others shun. Yeah.

Trumpets play triumphantly. Private X and Nobel-Committee Man shake hands, look official and smile for TV cameras. Then Private X grabs a surprised Nobel-Committee Man and kisses him on the lips. It becomes a prolonged kiss. Lights fade as trumpets become melancholic.

CHORUS
In a loud ominous whisper.
War and Peace, Peace and War
Married to each other for ever more. Whose Peace, Whose War?
Freeze.

Sancho (Jens Ochlast), Don Q
(Silvia Weiskopf) and the
Sodomites.

ACT III

—— SCENE 1 ——

Late afternoon. The Dead Sea. Salt rocks, earth, water. A science-fiction landscape. Lighting to match. A wall that moves, keeping them wanting more space. Don Q and Sancho outside a tent.

SANCHO

No breeze at all. But pleasant. What a strange world this is, Don Quixote. A touch of the Inquisition. Emperor Nero's rule in repetition. And this wall that seems to follow us everywhere so our space is being constantly restricted. I thought all walls had died in Berlin. This one seems alive. Is it a magic wall like the carpet of the Arabian Nights?

Wall moves closer. Don Q gives him a patronizing smile.

DON Q

Aside.

Sancho is not wrong. What a huge effort it is to live. Much worse is to celebrate one's decline with a regular display of fireworks. I loathe self-pity. To bemoan one's own fate while ignoring the evils in the world is to surrender everything. Or to imagine that because one is in love all is well with the world. Only a prostitute should be allowed to think like that. For the rest of us it's an escape from the pit, from the blood-red rain about to fall. Sancho is loyal and honest, qualities lacking in life, but that is not enough. Not for him. He finds it very depressing. I thought the sea air might cheer him up, but not this sea.

SANCHO

Don Quixote. How long will we stay here?

DON Q

As long or as little as we like. The sun has exhausted me. We need a siesta. Travel plans can wait till sunset.

They go into the tent just as Rocinante and Mule move centrestage.

MULE

Exciting isn't it?

ROCINANTE

What? Why?

MULE

I mean Old Testament country. It was in these parts that all the
great prophets stood and tended their flocks.

ROCINANTE

What in God's name have you been reading?

MULE

The Old Testament.

ROCINANTE

What's wrong with you? Everyone knows it's a compendium of
fairy tales.

MULE

Roci, before you start quoting Spinoza or Holbach I would like
to insist that, whatever else they might be, the Songs of Solomon
are not fairy tales.

ROCINANTE

Don't ever mock Spinoza. A few pages from him would cure you of your addiction to the Old Testament for ever because, despite what you sometimes say, you're not stupid. Your problem is you don't read enough! Spinoza told the rabbis to shove their orthodoxy wherever they wished. He would not change his opinions. They expelled him from the synagogue but mercifully no auto-da-fé. That's the privilege of the pope's batallions.

MULE

Stop. Stop. I will read Spinoza. Especially if he told his Inquisition to go stuff their injunctions up their arse.

ROCINANTE

Dear Mule. I can always depend on you to summarize important matters in a lofty and succinct fashion.

MULE

Than you, Roci. I'm flattered. But please answer my question. What are the Songs of Solomon?

ROCINANTE

Erotic love poetry. Humans need that sort of stuff to stimulate each other. They spend so much time trying to win the love of someone, but that's never enough. They have to waste more time. Praise heaven that we were not inflicted with all this nonsense. Lust is so much simpler. We see, we want, we jump. As for your Songs of Solomon. Author unknown. But I'm glad they put them into their Book. Wars, revenge, killings, tortures and burning of cities are not good for the nervous system of the superior species.

And yet, they carry on doing it. A casual flick of the switch and they could blow the whole world up today. The Songs were written for the interval between all the scenes of horror. We are different, but just this once let's dance to their tune?

ROCINANTE/MULE
'Let him kiss me with the kisses of his mouth—
for your love is more delightful than wine. Pleasing is the fragrance of your perfumes;
your name is like perfume poured out. No wonder the young women love you!
Take me away with you—let us hurry!
Let the king bring me into his chambers.'

They sigh in unison.

Lights fade and go out. Lute music, a starry sky. Sounds of singing and laughter. On the beach, the scene is lit with flaming torches.

—— SCENE 3 ——

All those assembled are wearing gowns with headgear of different colours. A rich mix. They are dancing with each other and with everyone. The men are slightly made up. They women are not. Don Q and Sancho watch from the side and then walk forward slowly. The music stops suddenly. Spotlight on the two men.

ORGANIZER
Stop. Who are you? Why are you here?

Others come forward and surround the men, admiring their clothes.

DON Q
We are travellers from a distant land. Don Quixote and Sancho Panza, at your service.

ORGANIZER
So word of our soirées must have spread far and wide. Are you two together?

SANCHO
Isn't that obvious?

Loud laughter.

ORGANIZER
No.

More laughter.

SANCHO

Oh Dios. I understand.

Whispers to Don Q, who bristles and draws his sword.

DON Q

Gentlemen, you have insulted me mortally. Your accusation that my squire and I are sodomites is a slander. We could be burnt if people believed you. It's disgusting. Are you all sodomites?

ORGANIZER

We are.

Don Q in a rage moves towards him with his sword as if to pierce him. Sancho runs up to him and restrains him.

DON Q

Why do you defile these sacred lands? This desert from which three religions emerged, this Eden of purity. Sodomite serpents steeped in sin, pestilential creatures, leave this region! Disappear! Or I will drive you out.

ORGANIZER

Smiling.

You sound like our rulers, men who oppress us. Is that your intention? Were you sent here by the Sultan of Saudia?

SANCHO

Sir, we are not used to the freedom you exhibit. We are travellers across time. We have seen much, but never a gathering such as this where you celebrate your vice without fear.

ORGANIZER

Without fear? Why do you think we're here? Its the only pace of safety. In our towns and villages, our love is hidden. We do not threaten men like you, but your aggression surprises me. Perhaps you are repressed but do not realize it. You think your arses are only there to shit. You deprive them of pleasures unforeseen. Even if you are a king, it's your arse that is the queen.

Loud laughter from the others. Don Q is very agitated, but realizes they are outnumbered and violence would be counterproductive. For the first time, he smiles.

DON Q

So this is your exile.

ORGANIZER

We did not mean to offend you. Pray, join our festivities. Eat and drink to your heart's content. We are all from this region, from cities big and small. We meet here once a year to celebrate without inhibitions. Our language may not be refined enough for you but our welcome is genuine. We cannot meet like this in any country.

DON Q

Thank you kind sirs, but I am still puzzled. I understand your orientation, but your party gear intrigues me. What is the occasion for this merriment?

ORGANIZER

Each year, we mark the birth of our great poet Abu Nuwas. Have you heard of him?

Sancho (Jens Ochlast), Rocinante (Ingrid Domann), Don Q (Silvia Weiskopf) and Young Poet (Tobias Roth).

DON Q/SANCHO
NO!

ORGANIZER

But you have heard of Sappho, of Michelangelo, Leonardo da Vinci. Alexander. Oscar Wilde. These names are known to you, but not Abu Nuwas. Let me put it simply: He is their equal. An Arab from Basra, where the beards now reign. An Arab from your ninth century. Go Google him and you will know. We can't teach you everything in one night. A brilliant poet, and gay. Like us. Every year, one of us is elected to play Abu Nuwas and preside over the event. Tonight, it is this young poet from Ramallah.

The Young Poet, a female dressed in mediaeval Arab clothes, steps out and bows to the visitors.

YOUNG POET

I was born and I died many centuries ago, in the time of our Caliph Harun ar-Rashid. You may have heard of him, if not of me. Have you read *Alf Layla wa Layla*? *A Thousand and One Nights*?

SANCHO

Indeed we have, Master Poet, and if you've read the book by Miguel de Cervantes, our creator, you would have observed how he absorbed the *Thousand and One Nights*. Perhaps you might even have heard of us.

CHORUS

Cervantes we have read, Cervantes we know. It may surprise you to hear we firmly believe he belongs with us in spirit, if not in deed. And for that reason, even if you are not TOGETHER, we welcome you as the children of the great Cervantes who knew our culture well. Welcome, Don Quixote and Sancho Panza, and may God bless your arses.

YOUNG POET

Let me show you our encampment. There is the Dead Sea, lower than this valley. We meet here because this is where the cities of the plain once existed. Gentlemen, you are standing on the exact spot where the Temple of Sodom once stood. Our sacred soil.

Don Q and Sancho stand petrified, clutching each other in fear.

TOGETHER

Sodom. God help us. Is that why you chose this place?

YOUNG POET

We celebrate the city destroyed by bigotry. We commemorate its citizens burnt to death. This year is special.

SANCHO

Why?

YOUNG POET

Look around you. Who are we? Our love can still not speak its name in our world. Introduce yourselves to our visitors and say where you're from.

DIFFERENT VOICES IN TURN

Abu Nuwas from Riyadh, Abu Nuwas from Doha, Abu Nuwas from Bahrain, Abu Nuwas from Cairo, from Basra, from Tehran, from Peshawar—a city filled with Abu Nuwases, Kabul, Sokoto, Timbuktu, Istanbul, Algiers, Tunis, Rabat.

CHORUS

Rabat? But the King is one of us. He once had a German lover. Together they rode the streets of the city in His Majesty's convertible car. Together . . .
Slight pause.
Together they rode each other. Together they rode each other.

SOLO VOICE

Abu Nuwas from the Vatican.

CHORUS

Abu Nuwas is the pope all dressed in pink,
A theologian who is not frightened to think,
But on this matter what he thinks he keeps to himself or shares only with a cardinal whom he has known for a long time. They read the Bible together.

DON Q

I am beginning to understand. But what you require is not a magic wand. You need to gather your strength. You need to have a plan.

CHORUS

This is why we're here. To discuss our plan in the heart of a city that would be ours if it existed. We are the children of Sodom and Gomorrah. We've been slandered long enough, persecuted, punished and killed. Why should we love in secret? It's not what Heaven willed.

YOUNG POET

Leviticus 20:13 leaves no room for doubt— 'If a man lies with a man as one lies with a woman, both of them have done what is detestable. They must be put to death; their blood will be on their own heads.' Here, all three religions are clear. Kill the arse-bandits.

The stage goes dark. Spotlight on a corner where the animals are resting.

ROCINANTE

Did you notice those camels pissing?

MULE

Yes.

ROCINANTE

But they were pissing backwards. Nobody in our species or the superior one does that.

MULE

Camels do. It shows that our species is more civilized. It's much more refined to piss backwards.

ROCINANTE

Not if there are others standing behind you.

Pause.

Our masters are worried about this place. Rightly so.

MULE

Why?

ROCINANTE

You know what happens in Sodom and if they're not careful . . .

MULE

Angry.

I'm really shocked by your homophobia. How the superior species pleasures itself is not our concern, provided they leave US alone.

ROCINANTE

That's what I really meant, Mule. This prejudice against same-sex love is relatively recent in the history of the superior species. It was the victory of the Big Three that is responsible.

MULE

Big Three?

ROCINANTE

Judaism, Christianity, Islam. They believed in a single god in the sky. Relaxed in Heaven but very harsh on Earth. Feuerbach understood . . .

MULE

Enough. Why do you always need a superior authority to buttress your arguments? This smart talk gets on my nerves. You're always showing off. Still a little insecure, perhaps? Sodom has been demonized for far too long. Lot betrayed his people, like collaborators have done throughout time. And these people gathered here today simply want to reclaim their history. They would have been better off when there was a world of many gods. No single authority.

ROCINANTE

Zeus, Athena, Apollo.

MULE

Wotan! Now he was something, and those Valkyries still give me
a tingle.

ROCINANTE

Venus, Mars, Cupid. Hermes?

MULE

No. Hermes was a pimp and a spy. Zeus' choir boy.

ROCINANTE/MULE

Prometheus! Prometheus! Prometheus!

MULE

Roci, there once was a religious leader who tried to help us.

ROCINANTE

Who?

MULE

Looks round and then whispers.
The late Ayatollah Khomeini.

ROCINANTE

You are losing your mind. The very mention of his name here
might bring on a drone attack.

MULE

I once went to a convention of donkeys and mules in a village
close to Tehran. They told me. The great Ayatollah had written in

his thesis that when he travelled through the countryside he came across many disoriented donkeys. When he asked the local members of the superior species as to why this was the case, they told him that the donkeys had been raped by many villagers.

ROCINANTE

How often?

MULE

That was not specified, but the Ayatollah expressed anger and wrote that good Muslims should not go about interfering with donkeys.

ROCINANTE

What about bad Muslims?

MULE

Or bad Catholics? Remember *Padre Padrone* by the Taviani brothers? The film set in Sicily . . .

ROCINANTE

And now who's using other authorities to broaden his case? Not me. Not me. Not me. And what else did you hear at the convention?

MULE

We ended by singing: Thank you, thank you, thank you for defending us, Ayatollah Khomeini, thank you very much . . .

Scene shifts to the whole stage. The full moon is out. The night is in progress.

A relaxed atmosphere. Everyone is laughing and enjoying a drink.
Don Q rises slowly to his feet.

DON Q

And this poetry you have been reciting by Abu Nuwas is scarcely
credible. Beardless young men with quivering, full buttocks? Even
though I find it distasteful in real life, the aesthetic is appealing.
Forgive my prejudices. I belong to a different generation.

YOUNG POET

Here's a last one before we turn to more serious matters:
'When my eyes roamed his cheeks as if grazing
In the Gardens of eternity, he said to me,
"Your gaze is fornicating with me!"
I replied: "Then my tears will give it the lash above
And beyond the legal prescription." '

Greeted with applause and a collective toast to 'Abu Nuwas, the Sultan
of All Poetry. We honour you on the day of your birth, Abu Nuwas.'

DON Q

When your evening started we were both sceptical. Perhaps Sancho less than I. His rural origins have made him far more
worldly. Now we perceive the dangers you face because of the

private lives you lead. Is now not the time to rebuild the smoke-blackened edifice here so cruelly destroyed by those who wrote the Old Testament? Did I hear one of you whispering earlier that the time had come? Speak. Let us share in this new project and sing its praises far and wide. Let not the dead weight of empires old and new and their local vassals obstruct you.

Drumbeats as all stand up holding the Sodom flag . . . a pink triangle on a green background

CHORUS

We the gay people of the Arab world, gathered here at the sacred site of Sodom, in order to encourage more perfect unions, establish Justice and Equality for all do hereby decide that we shall rebuild the city of Sodom. Its exact name, al-Sodomiyya, Sodomstaat or the Republic of Sodom—will be decided at a later stage by the citizens through a free vote. This city will be open to all those who are repressed, mistreated or simply depressed anywhere in the world. A sea without waves for a people tired of cruising.

Last sentence repeated three times with a hand gesture.

SANCHO

Dear friends, this is a truly inspiring occasion. You are founding a state based on the Old Testament. As you know, there are other examples so my advice is not to repeat the mistakes of the twentieth century.

CHORUS

We salute all righteous heterosexuals. We salute Don Quixote and
Sancho Panza. We salute our martyrs and forebears in history.
Saint Sebastian, Sappho, Abu Nuwas, Benedict Spinoza, Oscar
Wilde, Saint Teresa of Avila, Marie Antoinette, Abraham Lincoln,
Jean Genet and others too numerous to be named tonight but
whose names will be inscribed on the Wall of Remembrance
through which you will enter our city above the sea.

YOUNG POET

Brother Panza has advised us to avoid the mistakes of others. We
discussed this in some detail yesterday in various workshops and
there was general agreement on most issues. Let the workshop
representatives explain each decision in their own way.

WORKSHOP REPORTER 1

The social composition of the state of Sodom will prevent domination by any single ethnic, religious or non-religious grouping.
To forestall all possibilities such as attempts by Russians masquerading as gays to flood our new country and acquire it,
our Constitution will explicitly prohibit the domination by any
single ethnicity. All nations, all cultures, peoples, tribes will be
represented.

Applause.

WORKSHOP REPORTER 2

No standing army. We will not create an army masquerading as
the Sodom Defence Force. Elected popular militias will be suffi-
cient for local needs. If we are attacked we will appeal to CATO

and SATO, but never, never NATO. Never. Our visitors may not know this but CATO is the Chinese Arseholes Treaty Alliance which works closely with SATO . . . Sodom Arseholes Treaty Alliance. Together we can defend our borders.

Loud applause. Chants of 'CATO, SATO are more powerful than NATO.'

WORKSHOP REPORTER 3

However, given the military balance of the world, we will from this gathering onwards set in motion the creation of an America-Sodom Public Interest Committee—ASPIC—in New York and San Francisco, where support for our state will be huge and where International Gay Brigades will be rapidly created if we are ever threatened by reactionary, confessional, heterosexist states in this region. The first task of ASPIC will be to raise funds from sympathizers in factories and businesses in order to legally purchase via the lobby system at least a hundred members of the Congress and a dozen Senators. After that, the White House.

Applause.

WORKSHOP REPORTER 4

No pressure. No violence. Some gay people who live happily in different parts of the world will oppose this idea. That is their right. No pressure or threats, no bombing of bars that they frequent must ever be used to create a climate of fear in the heterosexual world. We will not force people to leave their countries just as we are building the new Sodom in an uninhabited area.

YOUNG POET

As to the economic character of the state, there was a long discussion but ultimately we all agreed that a single formula could be a founding principle of our Republic since it encompasses everything.

CHORUS

From each according to his ability, To each according to his need.

DON Q

We wish you luck. We wish you joy. Once ensconced in your new abode without the need to train men to kill, torture and die, without the need to build machines that vomit fire, death and destruction, you will be the envy of the world. Perhaps the gods of war, too, will discard their frightening masks and learn from you.

SANCHO

I would add my greeting to those of my friend, but if I may, without prolonging your activities much longer, ask a question that is not intended to be indiscreet. If Sodom is inhabited by males, where will the women go?

YOUNG POET

Dear friend Sancho, at the moment we are all together men and women.

Discards gown

And once we have built our Sodom on these ancient lands, we will build its sister city Gomorrah for women, but there is no intention of barring each from the other since there are many whose compass points in both directions. Sodom and Gomorrah will not be like ice and fire, but both ice and fire. On behalf of our people, farewell to our visitors and an invitation. You will be honorary citizens of our twin cities and always welcome here with your loyal animals whose intelligence we fear.

DON Q

If you wish to go forward, then hidden wisdoms you must learn.

Lights fade. Scene shifts to Somalia. Sand and sea.

Somali coast. Dark blue sea with waves.
Rocinante and Mule enter. Look at the audience. Then at sea.

ROCINANTE

The great Horn of Africa. Never thought we'd get here.

MULE

Why are we here?

ROCINANTE

My master was so excited by the news that new pirates were
roaming the seas again. It reminded him of the Barbary pirates.

MULE

I see. Pure sentimentality.

ROCINANTE

You're becoming very hard-hearted. Your character has changed during these adventures. As for sentimentality, you may be right but as Nietzche . . .

MULE

No. Fuck Nietzche! Enough name-dropping.

ROCINANTE

Listen, you ignoramus. We are in a continent that we once dominated. It was here that we, yes, WE permitted the superior species to emerge. This is the land of THEIR birth and who knows, perhaps THEIR death and ours.

MULE

Oh, don't be so morbid, Roci.

Enter Don Q and Sancho with Somali pirate as guide.

SANCHO

Where will the boat pick us up, Brother Pirate? Are we far?

Pirate points in the direction of the sea.

PIRATE

Another ten minutes. Were it not for this fog we would see it.

DON Q

Ah Sancho, isn't this incredible. Exploring parts we've never seen. Sipping coconut water with pirate friends. The questions we shall ask them are obvious.

The fog lifts. Dead bodies onstage.
Heaven protect us! What has happened here?

PIRATE

Warlords, Americans, Black Hawk Down, death, destruction.
That's why we fled to the sea. To live or, at least, to die with
dignity.

SANCHO

And Africa was once so close to us.

PIRATE

More people have died from wars and malnutrition on our continent over the last few years than the rest of the world put
together.

DON Q

Would it not be wonderful if we had the power to trap a day to
prevent it from becoming tomorrow? Or, better still, if we could
lay siege to tomorrow and prevent it from moving?

PIRATE

I feel safer on sea than on land. Africom, the bomber jets of the
rich world, are very active here. The French Papa with the tired
penis is sending more soldiers to our continent. A short war
to boost his image at home. We must hurry. I'm getting very
nervous.

*Before Sancho can reply, the stage darkens and a target shape forms
over their head. Two voices are heard.*

VOICE 1

We have the target. Somalian coast. Terrorist leaders on their way to join forces with sea pirates. Repeat. We have the target on computer. Permission to kill, Mr President.

VOICE 2

Permission granted.

Sound of approaching drone. The pirate runs as fast as he can offstage. Explosion. All goes dark. Silence.

SANCHO

Whispers.

Don Quixote, are you all right?

VOICE 1

Mission accomplished, sir.

Lights back on. Don Q is lying wounded, his head covered in blood. Sancho cleans himself up quickly and approaches his friend, puts his head in his own lap.

SANCHO

No, no. Not like this. Please God, not like this. Don't die, señor. You must live for many more years.

DON Q

When Achilles wept by the sea, Thetis, his silver-footed mother rose from the waves to comfort him. You are my only comfort, Sancho.

Sancho (Jens Ochlast)
and Don Q (Silvia Weiskopf).

SANCHO

This is not your fault. There is a power, strong and ugly, that dis-
poses of human lives as it sees fit. And it is not YOU, my friend.
Sometimes you behave as if you were God. Then you become Jesus
Christ. Now you've become Achilles. Stop all this immediately.

DON Q

I was wrong. It was this day that was marked, not the one that
will follow. Listen carefully, Sancho, and hold back that fountain
of tears. When we set out on our first adventure, I was mad. I
engulfed you in that madness and we were beaten, mistreated,
humiliated, but on this adventure I have been completely sane. It
is the world that is demented, on a path to self-destruction.

SANCHO

We have learnt a lot together, señor.

DON Q

That we always do, but usually when it's too late. We haven't let
anyone kick us around this time.

SANCHO

But they've killed you, señor. They've killed you.

DON Q

My one regret is that we will not be able to visit China together.
That is where the world might be remade. Might be. Might
be. Sancho, go East, my friend. And write the story of your
adventures.

SANCHO

It will not be the same without you.

DON Q

Remember when we were in Istanbul and we met a woman in
love with an exiled poet?

SANCHO

Nazim Hikmet, the Anatolian?

DON Q

The same. She recited a verse that I loved. I cannot recall it now.
On the edge of the sea in this continent of creation, I want to
hear it one last time before I die. Remember?
    'This earth will grow cold
        a star among stars
        and one of the smallest,
        a gilded mote on blue velvet—
        I mean THIS, our great earth.
    This earth will grow cold one day,
        not like a block of ice
        or a dead cloud even
    but like an empty walnut it will roll along
        in pitch black space . . .
    You must grieve for this right now
    —you must feel this sorrow now—
    for the world must be loved this much
    if you're going to say "I lived" . . .'
As they speak, the stage is filled with shadowy figures (the entire cast).

Don Q (Silvia Weiskopf)
and Sancho (Jens Ochlast).

DON Q

Who are all these people, Sancho?

SANCHO

I can't see anyone.

The figures draw closer.

CHORUS

We are angels sent to take you to Heaven . . .

DON Q

I am dying, and that knowledge brings clarity. I am not delusional. So alter your flight path, my friends. Bring Heaven down to earth.

He looks up at Sancho and dies. Pause. Silence. Lights out. A slight pause and then . . .

DON Q

Sancho, Sancho. Thank god this adventure's over. Could you book our flight to Shanghai today?